Praise for *Psychic Savvy*

Psychic Savvy offers a gold mine of practical ways to investigate our sixth sense. I have struggled with how to proceed on my own spiritual journey from time to time, and this illuminating book would have really helped. Ms. Englehart guides us on a path to self-discovery. Her straightforward style and ability to speak to every person's uniqueness, makes Psychic Savvy a seriously significant read.

Barbara Freas, Children's Writer and Educator

Psychic Savvy is a timeless and engaging handbook that makes for a fundamental daily read. The author thoughtfully conveys encouragement and understanding with a sprinkling of humor. This book addresses how to manage the challenges in life as well as our sixth-sense. Approachable and relatable with real-world nuggets of wisdom, Psychic Savvy will resonate with readers who want to create good in their lives. I wish I'd had this book 20 years ago.

Kelly Merritt, Author of the *Everything Guide to Family Budget Travel* and *Flight*

Psychic Savvy, Common Sense Answers to Your Psychic Reading and Development Questions

Copyright © Sheila Englehart (2019)

ISBN: 9781726877909

Requests to publish work from this book should be sent to: sheilaenglehart@gmail.com

Cover Art by www.StudioDesign.com

Psychic
Savvy

Common Sense Answers to Your Psychic
Reading and Development Questions

Sheila Englehart

Contents

My Story

Since childhood I had been obsessed with all things strange and unusual. I'd seen UFOs. I knew which houses were haunted. I could see and hear people that weren't living. And I traveled through the Bermuda Triangle three times just to know the mystery behind it, even if it swallowed me. (Not so much as a cloud or white cap in sight) My mother had a Ouija board that freaked me out a little. She went through a brief metaphysical exploration phase reading books by yogis and mystics, but she abandoned her search. Maybe because back then being psychic was still suspicious.

She believed that the things I mentioned were products of my overactive imagination, and that I was making them up. So, I stopped engaging with them. I went on to a traditional life of cubicle jobs, marriage, mortgage, etc. By the time I was thirty, I was lost -- spiritually bankrupt, struggling with my job and my marriage. I was utterly miserable, failing at everything, and no one could tell me why. Shrouded in depression, I was desperate to pull out of that dive.

On my morning commute, a local radio show hosted a psychic from Kansas. When Allene

Cunningham was in town, she would read the prospects of dreamers on air, then remind the audience that she'd be available for private readings over the weekend. She was The First Lady of Broadcast Psychic Counseling, but the advice she dispensed was practical, not mystical. I loved metaphysical ideas but was still a skeptic.

A couple days later, I met her at a hotel near the station. She looked exactly like she sounded – a cotton-headed grandmother. Her assistant warned me that her voice was failing because she wasn't feeling well. Not a promising introduction. After offering a couple of insights that didn't resonate, she said, "You need to read *The Power of the Subconscious Mind* by Dr. Joseph Murphy. That will help you tremendously."

My heart sank. *That's it? Read another book?*

I was already weary of reading books full of fluff by so-called experts. I'd spent real money on this session to come away with "read this book." How stupid and gullible was I?

But I was still lost. There was a bookstore on the way home. What was a few more bucks? I bought the paperback and wallowed in my disappointment.

Then I read it.

I was thrilled that it offered practical tools to help pull me out of my rut without resorting to self-medication or expensive therapy. It was a start. Allene also challenged my expectations of psychics as she did not offer any predictions on how life would turn out.

Our meeting took place 25 years before Ms. Cunningham left this life at 94. I cannot imagine where I might have landed had I not taken her advice. "Read this book."

The Suggested Reading and Resources section will have plenty for you to choose from.

What Being Psychic Means

Let's get one thing out the way. I am a writer, and I read tarot. I don't identify as being a psychic, but I use my sixth-sense all the time. And if you understand how your senses work, you'll realize that you do too. Or, you chose to allow your mind to override any intuitive impressions you do receive.

A few dictionary definitions of the word psychic include:

- A person receptive to outside forces
- Relating to the mind
- Capable of extraordinary mental processes
- Mental telepathy
- Pertaining to the mind - mental or spiritual
- Outside natural / scientific knowledge
- Sensitive to forces of a nonphysical nature

See anything weird or spooky there? It's not mind-reading or knowing everything about a person or situation. It means using your head along with data from your other senses.

But what pops into your head when you see the word psychic? Probably a fortune-teller from the movies pulling the death card to predict certain doom or a curse. That's entertainment for you.

What to Expect from a Psychic

Most people think a psychic is going to tell them what to do and how their situation or life will turn out. And sometimes they can, but few are really good at it. More often a psychic will offer data they receive, which may not be what the person wants to know. If they are attuned to your energy, they will offer information that is most important for you to know in that present time, not necessarily what you want to know for the long-term future. Expect to learn things for the short-term, then check in again down the road after some time (a few months) has gone by.

And if they offer predictions, they expect that you will remain on the path they see you on, taking steps toward your goals, not sitting on the couch waiting for what you want to ring the doorbell.

If a psychic tells you that you are cursed, and they can remove that for an additional charge, run. Run fast. Don't fall prey to their scare tactics. They are only "seeing" dollar signs.

You have the free will to accept or reject any information presented. You hold the power in your life, not the psychic. Now, want to develop your own psychic senses?

Where Do I Start?

Right Where You Are

Begin with the aptitude, knowledge, and beliefs you currently hold. Your circumstances, economic status, social class or religious affiliation have little to do with it. Spirit lives in all of us and has no status.

Where Are You?

You receive intuitive hits through your sixth sense all the time. Impressions come through your body's other five senses (sight, sound, touch, taste, smell). For centuries, traditional teachings by-passed this, but recently modern mystics have ushered it into the mainstream. Now there are plenty of resources available, and science is starting to find verifiable proof in quantum physics. Where are you?

> What are your natural talents?
>
> Where have you excelled?
>
> Better yet, what was your first personal psychic experience?

Identify How You Connect

When you get subtle intuitive hits or gut feelings that turn out to be right, how do they present themselves?

>Clairvoyance--seeing visions and dreams

>Clairaudience – hearing your Higher Self, guides and other beings

>Clairsentience – feeling--physical and emotional

>Clairsalience – smelling perfumes, food scents, or smoke with no visible source

>Clairgustance – information tasting "funny" or "bad."

>Claircognizance – knowing or prophecy-- It's just there.

What Attracts You?

Spirit communication? Divination? Energy healing? Art? Figure out what attracts you and learn as much as possible about it.

Practical Approach

For those who want a Step-by-Step,

1. Learn Psychic Protection

. . . along with how to clear your energy field. A column of white light (from the Divine source) is not always enough for all circumstances. Have a variety of protection and grounding techniques in your toolbox.

2. Study with a Tool

Tools help engage the conscious mind while opening the subconscious to connect with the Divine. What attracts you? Tarot, astrology, crystals, numerology, art, dowsing, etc. Find an expert and immerse yourself in their books, classes, and techniques.

3. Practice Daily

Practice grows proficiency. Integrate it into your life with other practices like meditation, exercise, altar and ritual work, automatic writing or journaling, channeling, etc. Create sacred time and space for regular practice.

4. Commit to Your Spirit

Your human spirit has been ignored long enough. With a commitment to honing your skills, you will expand your spirit and elevate others with your light energy and intuition.

Change seems to have accelerated in the past few years. Climate, political unrest, and societal priority shifts have activated abilities lying dormant in people: seeing the dead, telepathy, heightened empathy, sensing illness in others, prophetic visions of future events to name a few. Developing your abilities can only help you grow with these changes.

Motive

Having another sense provides an advantage. But what is your true motive for using it?

Spiritual Motives:

- Know your own heart and spirit.
- Foster self-respect, peace, and inner harmony.
- Align with nature and the external environment.
- Connect to your true belief system.
- Reconnection with the Oneness of humanity.
- Make more decisive decisions.
- To better serve the world.

Egotistical Motives:

- Material wealth
- Fame (television show, bestseller, etc.)
- Power with Social or Professional Status

Ego is that willful, confident, magnificent part of self that propels you toward your goals. But feeding only the ego can overshadow your lighter spirit. If you develop your abilities only for money and fame, your psychic door can close before you can say, "But wait!"

7

Take it from music mogul Quincy Jones, if your motive is solely money, "God leaves the room."

If your intention is to bring the best energy to everyone involved, you are in service to yourself as well as others.

No Secret Formula

No shortcuts. You must do the work.

But here's my stab at a formula:

Connection + Intention + Action = Creation

Get your mind still enough to *connect* to your spiritual source, focus your *intent*, then take *action* toward your creation. Not a quick process.

You must commit to spending time doing the work with sacred intention, then relax enough to let the connection occur. You are developing a muscle that hasn't had a lot of exercise. It's an energetic workout that takes time, repetition, and patience.

Religious people call this connection "trusting God" or "listening to your soul." Whenever you hear someone say, "God told me" or "I was led by the Holy Spirit," they were connecting to their Higher Self or spiritual center.

Creation begins with your first breath of intention; then your project is continually in various stages of development.

But, before you begin any psychic practice, it's essential to protect yourself.

Psychic Protection

Before you attempt to connect you must know "as above, so below." In other words, if you believe in a higher power, you must understand there is also a lower one to balance it.

Protect Yourself Before Opening a Door to the Unknown

If you wouldn't go into a snowstorm without a coat, or go into battle unarmed, you shouldn't head into the unknown realms of the Other World without energetic protection.

Consequences to Carelessness

Unwanted energy can stick to you. The psychic connection can be a beautiful "love and light" experience, but without protection, it can be as cautionary as unprotected sex.

Ignorance Isn't Bliss

There is so much we don't know about the unknown and unseen. It is crucial for you to armor up--create an energy shield, call on spirit protectors, and use physical tools.

> *To those on anti-depressant medication. Medications are prescribed to control and enhance mood.*

You should not attempt "light" work if you are mentally or emotionally in a "dark" place.

To those feeling physically unwell. *While your physical body is in a healing state processing virus or infection, it is best not to attempt any psychic work until you have returned to feeling back in balance.*

A spirit board like Ouija is marketed as a game but can also act as an open door or gateway to the Other World. The Living World is full of duality. Assume that the Other World is as well. Luck favors the prepared. There is no list of cautions on the box, so it's best if an experienced, spiritually reverent facilitator is present to guide you through rules, ethics, and prayers for protective assistance. This person acts as a gatekeeper and the voice of reason. It's also good practice to end the conversation by thanking the energies who communicated through the board and close the connection. Think of this as getting their coats and seeing them to the door after their visit.

Cautionary Tale: I met a teenager who spent a lot of time with the Ouija app on her phone, and she had unknowingly opened a floodgate. Spirits were tormenting her, not letting her sleep, and making aggressive contact. Any device with a battery or electrical power only amplifies the energy. With assistance, she had to bid them farewell, send them back through the gate, learn protective boundaries, and delete the app from her phone.

Learn All You Can

Do your research before beginning any practice and ask an experienced person to lead the session, not a friend who saw it on TV.

How do you **clean and protect your energy field** from invisible energies?

Smudging is a temporary space cleansing technique, but not strong enough to banish negative energies for good. White sage acts more like disinfectant. If you go out into the world, you may bring home hitch-hiking energies. Smudging should be a regular practice, either burning or spraying.

Amulets are also nice for personal shielding, but not the only tool you'll need. An amulet only has power if you believe it does. Charge it with your energy. Know that you also must protect the rest of your energy field, especially your back.

Column or Bubble of White Light is fabulous but not necessarily an all-in-one solution for everyone. For those rooted in a solid spiritual belief system, this can be more than enough. But what if you haven't figured out what you believe?

Evaluate Your Beliefs

Where do you believe that light or connection comes from? You can do this through visualization, ritual, prayer, music, and consistent programming. Research, then experiment with what works for you. I love visualization. If I'm sitting in a chair, I imagine that I turn on a lamp and the beam of light puts me in the spot. I ask that the White Light of the (Great Spirit, Christ Consciousness, Universe, God, Goddess) surround and protect me.

If I'm exposing myself to a crowded environment, I add more protection around the light. If I place myself inside a bubble of light, then I surround that with onion-like layers of color, sound, razor wire or saw blades that I set in motion. I use an image like the machine from the film *Contact*. One layer can move clockwise, the next layer counterclockwise, the next front to back.

Isn't That My Imagination?

Imagination creates our reality through thoughts, words, and imagery. Every innovative tool in our world began as an idea in someone's imagination before action was taken to bring it to fruition.

Your idea can be as simple or complex as you like if it helps you feel protected. If I am in a rush to pop into a store, I visualize pulling an Invisibility Cloak over my body like Harry Potter or I'm zipping up an energetic wetsuit. When I emerge from the store, I imagine shedding the garment and placing myself in a white tornado. As I walk to the car, I see any negativity or residual energy flinging off me.

Movement can help you shake unwanted energies. Wind can blow away germs and debris, even move mountains. Dance. Jump up and down. Bound on a trampoline. (It's hard to remain angry while you're bouncing.) A brisk walk, a run, cycling, rowing, bashing a tennis ball across a court, or any movement can dislodge energy like a bug on a windshield. And re-energize you.

Music is movement through the airwaves that alters your energy and allows you to feel lighter. Next time you're angry or depressed, put on your happy music. You may find it difficult to remain in that state of mind.

Water is a great cleanser. Taking a shower after a hard day not only washes the skin but the energy field. Having a soak in Epsom or sea salts also neutralize energies. Be sure to submerge your head too. When you're done, visualize all the unfriendly junk going down the drain.

Entertainment like comedy can lighten you up. Be selective. But entertainment media is not a trusted resource of information. Drugs, natural disasters, political upheaval bring heavy energy. Even our computers get viruses. We consume most information through media today and it's easy to forget that entertainment does **not** have any responsibility to be accurate. It's escapism, not knowledge.

Hit The Books. Look to your local library. Secret mysteries and traditions can now be found on the shelves. How-to manuals and periodicals on everything you've ever wondered about are readily available. But some should have safety warnings to "consult a professional before trying at home." With life accelerating, we all want to skip right to the list of instructions without learning proper precautions. Imagine if your doctor or pharmacist did that.

Want an **iron-clad method** of protection?

I recommend the PDF download of the Archangel Metatron Prayer of Protection and Abundance from Michelle Whitedove--
www.michellewhitedove.com/links-recommendations

Your Energy Field

Create and Maintain Your Energy

Thoughts, words, beliefs, attitude, and emotions – they're all in your personal energy field. You can wake up in the morning with low energy, then boost it with a shower, exercise, or breakfast. When you arrive at work to chaos, your energy shifts again, along with your mood. Your thoughts and attitude change with your circumstances and situations.

Think about grief. We don't need to see someone dressed in black with a fixed gaze to recognize their emotional state. Their energy is so low that they are almost invisible -- a ghost of their former selves. They haven't eaten or moved much. They haven't exposed themselves to external stimuli, listened to music, or made social connections. They feel sedate as if a part of them has died.

Changes in your state of mind alter your energy and ripple outward. Even if you keep your thoughts to yourself, your energy will communicate through emotion and body language.

When you present yourself to the world, even when you wear a protective mask, be aware of the energy you bring with you. No one can be bubbly and joyful all the time. When you're angry, you can choose to shift your energy to be more accommodating. You don't have to remain in a bad mood all day if your morning started with spilled coffee, screaming kids, and traffic crawl. Some things in life are out of your hands, but you can control your reaction to them. You are in the driver's seat of your own life, even when you feel powerless to shift your circumstances.

Your Own Worst Enemy

A well-meaning neighbor wanted me to go on a blind date with her friend. I hadn't recovered from my last relationship and wasn't ready to date. Then guilt kicked in and I didn't want to seem ungrateful. To make her happy, I went against my better judgement. It did not go well.

When you go against your first impression, it can spell disaster. If you haven't healed or freshened up your energy to align with others, you can end up feeling like an ink stain on white linen.

Pleasing others is great if that means you don't have to compromise what you know is best for you. Make choices based on your own feelings and you'll save yourself and others a lot of frustration.

You Have the Power to Change Your Energy

Thoughts, movement, social interaction, entertainment, or any activity that lightens you up gives you control. It mingles with others unintentionally and invisibly. Keep it light, and you can help lift someone else up a notch or two. A smile can be the most surprising tool in darkness. You have the power.

Where Attention Goes, Energy Grows

If you are angry, your energy field grows full of negativity. If you are joyful, it might expand with delight and pleasure.

When someone else's energy bleeds into yours, it can leave sticky energy prints. If you take public transportation, you instinctively pull your energy close to your body so that it doesn't trespass onto others. You can also expand your energy field when you have a presentation or need to be seen. You feel it through eye contact, and body language. Some speakers exude a ton of energy, and others put you to sleep. Watch a comedian perform and you'll see how large their energy grows with the audience response. Politicians, religious leaders, self-help teachers know how to expand their energy field to reach millions.

Fuel Your Intentions

You get up in the morning with a list of things you need to accomplish, while also having personal dreams and desires. You need to have enough energy after your day job and family time to chip away at personal goals.

Chakra Energy Centers

The primary seven chakras are energy wheels or power centers that run from the base of your spine to the crown of your head. The first three deal with the physical body, the top three correspond with the spiritual body while the heart chakra acts as the bridge between them. These orbs of energy move (or not) in connection with your physical body to your spiritual awareness.

Chakra 1 – Base/Root--red – (I Am)--physical security

Chakra 2 – Sacral--orange – (I Feel)--creativity and sexuality

Chakra 3 – Solar Plexus--yellow – (I Do)--personal power in action

Chakra 4 – Heart--green – (I Love)--emotion and connection

Chakra 5 – Throat--blue – (I Speak) – communication/expression

Chakra 6 – Third eye--indigo – (I See) – intuition, perception

Chakra 7 – Crown--violet – (I Know)--spiritual understanding

Learning to clear, strengthen, and utilize your energy centers can help you stay balanced with one foot on the ground and one foot in Divine connection.

There are volumes of books on the chakra energy system. Tori Hartman has made chakras her life's work and created the amazing *Chakra Wisdom Oracle Cards* and companion books. Kala Ambrose's *Awakened Aura* is also high on my list.

Grounding

Grounding is a term for your Spirit re-entering the physical body after you've opened to high-level energy or astral-traveled. Bliss Bunnies are so happy being out-of-body they don't want to return to the heavy physical state. Re-engaging with the Earth brings you back like landing a plane after a short flight.

Send unwanted energy into the ground through your feet or burn off energy with movement, sunlight, music, salt bath, or time in nature.

Ways to Ground:

Eating or drinking (healthfully)

Showering/bathing

Walking barefoot on natural earth

Inhaling citrus, lavender, and mint scents

Touching a tree or plant

Picking flowers or fruit – gardening or digging in the dirt

Visualizations that send energy through your feet into the ground

Energy Vampires

You Can Charge Another's Battery

We all know people rooted in their troubles. You grant them your time, listen to their woes, offer advice that they overrule with "That won't work because . . ." It's exhausting, even if you don't keep up with all their drama. They don't value your time or attention because it's all about them. And after they've laid all their burdens on you, they'll say, "I feel so much better now." They have unintentionally drained your battery and even imprinted some of their depression, anger, and chaos onto you.

Strangers Can Be Silent Thieves

The energy of others can linger or leave traces like soot. Ever come out of a public place feeling awful? A headache, stomach ache, any pain or discomfort you didn't have before you went in? As soon as a lighter, brighter, unsuspecting soul happens through, those energies are drawn to stick to you like toilet paper on your shoe.

They don't need to consciously engage with you. Places with an inflow of humanity can feel uncomfortable, even unsafe. Hospitals and doctor's offices where people might be sitting in fear can feel especially unnerving. Standing in line at the market or waiting at the DMV exposes you.

Energy Leaves Residue

Clearing your energy is as important as washing the dishes or cleaning your bathroom. Just as you wash your hands often in cold and flu season, adopt the same habit in your energy field. Energy deposits can be as toxic as the humans who left them.

Take anger. Even if you're not part of an argument, fragments can splatter onto your energy field like bleach spots on your favorite jeans. Witnessing a horrific event can do damage. Violence can leave an emotional imprint. Accidents, natural disasters, movies, and TV shows can snag your energy like delicate fabric.

Expand and Shrink Your Energy

If you are standing in line at the market, allow for personal space. If someone snuggles too close to you, you may want to put up your energy barrier of protection.

I used to be annoyed when someone stood too close for comfort. I'd take a step, and they'd move with me. After learning light work, I realized they were unconsciously drawn to my energy, like warming by the fire. No one comes close if I'm not in light mode. If my energy is angry or chaotic, people give me a wide berth.

If you encounter people daily, you must learn Psychic Protection to prevent the unconscious draining or attachment of unwanted energy.

Retrieve Your Soul Fragments

With every exchange of energy, we exchange soul fragments. When the exchange is especially negative or hurtful, it is essential to retrieve your fragments as well as returning any that you unconsciously took from the other party. There are complicated techniques for doing so, but I prefer simply asking for them to gently return to me or their originator. You can ask Archangel Michael to help cut any cords attached.

Learn Cord Cutting

Every contact you have with another creates a cord of connection like a strand of webbing from a spider. Do a visualization to cut cords of attachment so that their energy does not influence you in a negative manner. Salt and other physical tools can be used as well. Cord cutting make take several times to complete. This is especially useful after a bad break-up.

Choice

You Decide

Some of us are expected to follow in family footsteps. Others are supposed to be caregivers or marry well. We might be programmed to serve our family, country, and community without the benefit of independent opinion or choice. As adults, we are free to make our own choices. But it might take years to figure out who we are and what we want apart from the expectations and influences of others.

Your Free Will

In a free country, no one has the right to bully you into doing what you don't desire. Are you aligned with your desires? As ever-changing creatures of free will, our desires and goals will also change. You are the best judge of what is right for you. A tarot or astrology reader can show you the qualities you bring to the table, insight, an aptitude perhaps, but it's not the job (or responsibility) of any reader to make decisions for you. If you still want to be told what to do with your life, there are plenty of authority figures willing to oblige. Remember that you have the right to change your mind should their advice not feel right.

Divination tools can offer possibilities, none of which are carved in stone. For those who believe in destiny or what is written, that doesn't mean you don't have choices. It also doesn't mean that you are prepared to take the path you want when you desire to. I know all about impatience. What slows us down is our haste to do things to move farther, faster.

But isn't that intention?

No. That is the desire to have what you want when you want it. Intention allows for patience, experience, and right timing.

Know *What* You Want and *Why* You Want It

People able to propel themselves faster are clear on what they want and what they were willing to do to get it. With clear intention, we make faster choices but still require right timing. Some people seem charmed -- everything they touch seems to fall into place with little or no effort. They are energetically aligned to a specific intention, conscious or unconscious.

The rest of us struggle to find our true path, groping around in the dark until we find a door to try because we don't have clarity on what we want or what we are willing to do for it.

And timing? Your right timing may be different than others. You may follow every step of a successful achiever only to fail. Remember, outliers make success look easy.

Stay in the Present

If you always look to the future, you miss the present. Most of us are so desperate to know *what will be* that we don't see *what already is*. Life happens right here and now. These here-and-now moments comprise your life. Everyone's measure of success is different. It's up to you to put the work into your choices. With a little luck and right timing, success can find you.

No One Gets a Pass

Our spirit doesn't choose a human incarnation to have a trouble-free life. Its intention is to experience specific aspects. Just as no medical student chooses to spend twelve years or more training to be a doctor because they think it will be easy. Life is a collage of experiences and choices. And we can view it as our Heaven, or hell, or somewhere in between. Most of all, life is an education. How far we advance will be based on choices. Maybe we'll drop out early, enlist in the military, move to a foreign country, play pro ball, or get more than one doctorate. When we feel we've done all we want to, we move on.

28

Bless the Difficulties

The hard times are the greatest opportunities to learn lasting lessons. Those who breeze through some areas of life will struggle in others. No one, no matter how rich, famous or powerful, has it easy in every aspect of their lives. Envy of another is a waste of time and energy. Focus your intentions on *your* growth and development. In other words, mind your own business so you can grow your way.

Choices You Make and Choices That Make You

I was a horrible test taker in school. I second-guessed a lot of my answers. Is that a trick question? Did I read it correctly? Most of the time I changed an answer only to find my first answer had been correct. First impressions are usually right. Had I trusted mine, I would have scored better on my SATs and perhaps chosen a different direction.

Your Mind Isn't Always Smart

Your head can give you reasons why or why not like a salesperson convincing you *this (choice, product) is the smarter choice,* when your internal voice screams, *"Nooooo!"*

You've made many decisions that probably went against your gut because your friends and family advised it was the smarter thing to do.

If you learn to trust your emotional-self more than your intellectual-self, you will make more *right* choices. With practice, you'll feel your body signals and give those the proper attention. Feeling helps develop trust.

Trust Takes Time

. . . and patience. Begin with simple choices every day. What do I want for lunch? What does my body want? What does my mind think is best? Your body might want something green and clean while your head is full of cheeseburgers and fries. What to do? Pay attention to how your body feels after each question. Catalogue it all.

Or you can learn to muscle test or use a pendulum.

Muscle Testing

To muscle test, link your index fingers and thumbs together like lobster claws. "Yes" means you shouldn't be able to easily pull them apart. "No" means the link should break without much effort. Sounds silly, but it works for many.

While you are practicing with yes or no questions, feel your body. What is your stomach doing when your fingers are giving "yes" answers? Run through your body's responses: chest, spine, stomach, and skin. Note what happens after each question. Feelings are subtle, which is why your head can so easily override your physical sensations. Your mind must be still enough to hear it, feel it, see it, smell it, taste it, or know it.

Pendulum

No time? I love using a pendulum. It's fast, efficient, and versatile. Once you are proficient, you can use your body's subtle movements as a substitute.

What if I make the wrong choice? There are only right choices at that moment, based on current circumstances, situations, needs, and desires. A choice made the next day or any other moment might be different. Once you make a choice, stick with it.

Oh, and *not* making a choice is a choice.

Want to learn the pendulum from the best? Take a class from Raymon Grace--
www.raymongrace.us

Belief

You Are What You Believe

If it walks like a duck and quacks like a duck, is it a duck?

Imposters are everywhere pretending to be something they are not. Who do you think you are? If you believe that you are a worthless nobody, that is how the world will see you until you change that thinking. But believing you are above the law or untouchable doesn't always make you so. Generally, you become whatever you are programmed to be by authority figures. After you mature enough to make your own decisions, you have the power to change the loop in your mind. But it takes will and time.

What do you believe?

Where is your divinity? Is there a deity who governs all? Do you really have free will? Is everything pre-destined? Is there life after death or a restful dirt nap? Do you believe in yourself and your abilities? Do you believe you are different from the rest of the population?

Most of us believe in *something* but what? It might not match conventional wisdom. Your beliefs are as unique and specific to you as your iris or your fingerprints. Not even twins are exact. Your beliefs grow and change as you do.

You Don't Need a Specific Belief

You have everything that you need inside to create what you choose. If you believe that you are spiritual being, imagine that connection as an energetic thread or power cord. You have only to plug in to the Divine.

Your Mind is Like a Computer

Your hard drive saved everything you've ever heard, felt, smelled, tasted, spoken, and experienced. As a child, you absorbed, accepted, and filed away all that data. Most of your ideas began as someone else's. As you matured, you used it as raw material to reshape as your own. I recommend deleting the mental "cookies" from your inner hard drive with meditation.

Believe You are Part of the Whole

If you believe in the power of a psychic connection, you must believe in a Divine source of which you are a small particle.

Namaste. *The light in me honors the light in you*.

No matter what personal insecurities you may possess, what your peers or parents say, what your boss thinks, accept that you are a spiritual being.

Claim that. Believe that. Imagine that you are a pure human spirit before anyone impressed any outside opinions and beliefs onto you.

Believe in Yourself

Belief in self is the hardest, most powerful process of any self-development. You have value and ability. You influence and affect the world around you. You create energetic ripples that spread outward with every action you take in every connection you make. What you believe about yourself matters.

Respect Yourself

Self-respect may be a big challenge. Your thoughts have had years of downloads from others. You can reprogram unhealthy thinking with consistent awareness.

Imagine that you are a pack mule. People are packing all their stuff onto your back. Not only will you be carrying that weight, but you'll be stuck listening to their complaints, worries, doubts, and beliefs as they lay their burdens on you. You may not understand their language, but you'll feel their frustration or emotional energy.

Programming is Sneaky

Ask anyone in advertising. Commercials are designed to convince you that you need their product. That data is stored in your subconscious. Be selective about which information you consume.

Believe That You are Creative

"Oh, I'm not creative."

We all are. Don't mistake creativity for old-school art like drawing, painting, music, and crafting. Creativity is a force. How do you think we sent a man to the moon? Where did we get our advanced technology on all our laptops, tablets, and Smartphones?

You may have created a home, family, business, closet, a haven for strays, beauty, and serenity, protocols or classes in your field. You have created a way of life for yourself that evolves as you do.

Examine your beliefs. What was passed down from your family, church, peers, and community? How many do you still hold true? All of these are a part of your programming until you delete them from your inner hard drive. Which programs no longer serve you?

Believe That You Matter

Spirit has no status. No matter your flaws, foibles, fears or station in life, you are worthy of spiritual connection. No matter who has tried to convince you otherwise. You matter.

Your Spiritual Team

Who do you talk to when you're alone? Where do signs, omens, and other signposts come from? God/Goddess, Higher Self, an oracle, angels, guides, aliens, or woodland creatures? That depends on your belief system.

Many a successful person had a champion in their corner. If you don't have an emotional support team on the ground, lean on your mystical spirit team. Just because you can't see them doesn't mean they aren't right behind you waiting for you to ask. Not what you believe? Then trust your sacred self, inside and out.

The Universe is vast, and you are a tiny organism in it. Even if you don't believe in a specific energy, trust that you don't know everything. Saying a simple, yet sincere "Thanks" is all that is necessary.

Angels

I used to think angels were beings that humans dreamed up to not feel alone. Then I saw one. Scared the oatmeal cookie out of me. It was gigantic and stoic. I felt like a small dog in comparison.

Angels are a unique species of light being. Deceased loved ones may assist like angels can, but they are not pure light. According to religious texts, only Metatron and Sandelphon had human incarnations before becoming angels.

Angels don't care if you know their names or what they do. They abide by the Law of Free Will and cannot intercede without your request unless your life is in danger. In general, they need your consent to work on your behalf.

There are all kinds of rituals designed for this, but all you need to do is ask as you would any friend – out loud or in writing. But you must ask. If you don't speak aloud (even whisper) or write it out, these thoughts cannot be separated from your innermost monkey-mind. Angels must know what you need help with and that thought can get lost in the millions of others you have daily. Nothing is too big or too small, yet I'm never comfortable asking for little things of such powerful beings. Remember to be specific without being limiting.

Angels can present themselves in any form aligned with your personality and belief system - helpful human to happy animal to shady tree.

Spirit Guides

Animal, Vegetable, People

Spirit guides come in a variety of forms, each having had an incarnation on Earth and graduated to an elevated degree of service. The plant and animal kingdoms are connected to us as living beings and communicate in their own language as well. Be open to their guidance.

Guides change or tag-team according to our needs. I like to believe there is one manager in who delegates to my other guides. I don't have to know specifically who is with me. They seem to know what I need before I do. They can present physical signs, whisper in your ear, prompt sensations in your body, trigger emotions that covertly keep you on the path that you have set for yourself. If you decide to change your path, you can ask for their help.

Just Ask

This can sound like they are genies that grant wishes. And sometimes, when you get immediate responses to your requests, it can feel that way. You might not always get what you ask for in the time you'd like it. More likely, you get what you need. They need enough time to set things up behind the scenes while you take action.

Consider it a team effort where they hold a couple extra cards to play.

Guides show up when and how we need them. Still, you must request their help and permit them to do so. Then be open and patient in waiting for a response. When you work with a living person give your guides permission to work with their guides in a team-effort.

Ask, then pay attention to signs, synchronicities, and sensations to feel your next step.

Your Spirit

You are a Spiritual Being and Team Leader

It's your life. It is up to you whether you take cues from your team, or not. Ultimately, all decisions are yours. The team members can offer signs, open pathways, even give you a shove. As an independent spirit, you create your energy and make the choices. The buck starts and stops at you.

There are times when you think your team is no help at all. Maybe you've been leaning on them for everything. They might even mislead you to snap you out of dependence so that you can stand on your own occasionally. They may know things we don't, but they aren't you. They don't have to live your life.

Honor your spirit! You are part of the tapestry of the world. Without you in it, the world would be different. Your ripples touch more than you'll ever know.

Connection - Body

How do I connect to spiritual energy? By first balancing body and mind.

Take Steps Toward Optimal Health

There is no one-size-fits-all approach to your body. But to take a spiritual journey, you must take proper care of the vehicle you are using to get there. If you are climbing a mountain, you need to be in good shape to reach the top, along with having tools for survival. If you are physically imbalanced or unwell, the journey will be much more difficult. You might be terribly out of shape or have severe asthma or allergies. The climb will be tough if you are carrying excess baggage or have difficulty breathing. Best to get as healthy as you can before you begin.

You Are What You Ingest

I don't subscribe to the idea that you must be vegan to be spiritual. I'm more of an everything-in-moderation kind of girl. But I do know that the closer you eat to nature, the closer you are to the spirit of the Earth. If you self-medicate with sugar or consume stimulants or chemicals in excess, your body will weaken. Best to be as nutritionally sound and physically healthy to connect to the

Other Worldly frequencies. Maintain optimal health for your body and find the protocol specific to your needs.

If you want to connect to the "Spiritual" network, do you want a weak device like a cheap phone? Or would you prefer the best equipment?

> Being out of shape or unwell doesn't mean you can't access Spirit. It only means it might be more challenging. There is always more than one way to do anything. Commit to becoming your personal best. You'll need to get comfortable with patience and discipline or at least tolerant of them.

If you haven't seen Louise Hay's *You Can Heal Your Life*, check it out. It's still a reference I reach for. I am also fond of Anthony William's books like *Medical Medium.* He is very much a modern Edgar Cayce.

Connection - Mind

Develop a Quiet Mind

. . . so that stillness can speak. How do you achieve stillness?

Meditation

"But I can't meditate!"

You do it all the time without realizing it. Ever zone out? Stare into space? Someone will ask, "What are you thinking?" You'll say, "Nothing."

Gaps between unfocused thought and feeling are where connection occurs. That space is *subtle.* It's not loud or black and white.

Think of the Divine as an infinite satellite connection. The human spirit can connect to that energy and data like a computer or phone can connect to the web.

Having a quiet mind doesn't mean you won't have any thoughts, only that you will be able to *detach* from them. Think about people you pass in the market. Perhaps you smiled or spoke to them without memory of the encounter. You can do that same with thoughts that demand your attention. Nod and move on. In your meditation space, you should have a boundary to hold back daily demands until you finish your quiet time. Bat thoughts away like beach balls or leave them with your shoes outside the door.

Meditate in Moments

You can meditate in the shower, waiting for your toast, your flight, or walking the dog. It's great if you can create the ideal setting – comfortable position, no distractions, and complete safety-- but how often do you find that? It is far more beneficial to be able to meditate anytime, anywhere--from a park bench to a busy airport. One of the objects of meditation is to train your consciousness to be still no matter what is going on in your life. From personal drama to trouble at work, you can do a quick meditation to restore calm.

Silence is Not Always an Option

The world is noisy. City folks might find the sound of sirens, banging trucks, and puffs of diesel air brakes soothing. Silence might drive them bonkers. Meditation is a peaceful state of mind, not necessarily a quiet place.

On the flipside, what is your daily level of noise exposure? Do you wear earbuds to block out the rest of the world? If clairaudience is your dominant sense, noise might block the flow or distract from any incoming intuitive information.

Walking without earbuds or music can help settle your mind even in the presence of other ambient sounds. Consider periodically unplugging from all media, even music. All the to-do lists, conflicts, and daily demands swirling around your busy brain might get a chance to land.

You can do chores and clean your mental closets at the same time. Focus on the activity.

Breath as Meditation

Sidetracked or anxious? Take a few moments to breathe to a count. In through your nose, out through your mouth.

Taking a test? Performing? Appearing in court? Breathe to a count. If you count backward slowly from 10 down to 1, visualizing each number as you go, you can clear your mind.

When you are nervous, frustrated, or angry, the fastest way to regain control is to breathe deeply from your solar plexus. Belly breathing helps you gain a mental hold of your thoughts to ease any emotional triggers. Focus on breath will distract you from thoughts vying for your attention. Breath has rhythm like a dolphin surfacing for air. Breathe, dive, exhale while rising to the surface.

Inhale through your nose to a count, hold to a count, exhale through your mouth to a count. Eventually, you won't have to count, and you'll be able to incorporate other intentions to your meditations.

Find the Light

With your eyes closed, "look" where you would imagine eight feet from your third eye to be. Watch for the light to appear on that dark horizon. The longer you watch, the pin-prick of light will grow into a bright sun. Be patient. Practice.

Dr. Andrew Weil's 4-7-8 Video

https://www.drweil.com/health-wellness/body-mind-spirit/stress-anxiety/breathing-three-exercises/

Repeating a Mantra

Repeating OM silently or aloud can provide your mind a landing space. If it's busy repeating OM, it's not distracted by thoughts.

Dr. Wayne Dyer's *Meditations for Manifesting* uses this same technique with "AH" instead of OM.

Stare at the Moon

You can clear a busy mind by staring at the moon for a few minutes. Try to keep your neck and shoulders relaxed and your gaze focused on the moon. Breathe.

The Violet Flame

Repeating this mantra from *The Violet Flame to Heal Body, Mind, and Soul* by Elizabeth Claire Prophet invokes an all-encompassing force that heals and transmutes negative energies.

I AM the violet fire, the purity God desires.

YouTube.com has many guided Violet Flame meditations. Find one you like.

Visualization

Brain Squeeze. Imagine that there is a lid on top of your head that you can open to access your sponge-like brain like a cartoon. Imagine that you can lift the lid and remove your brain, submerge it in a bucket of soapy water and squeeze out the excess thoughts, worries, and emotions like mud. Repeat this imagery until your brain squeezes clean.

Blackboard cleaning. Imagine your mental blackboard covered with all your thoughts, worries, and emotions. You can barely read it. Take a wet sponge and wipe it clean, dunking it in a bucket of water and wringing it out with every swipe. (Any dirty surface would work: dishes, windows, floors, cars, etc.)

Simplicity can bring peace. The simpler your activities, the calmer you remain.

There are tons of meditations to choose from-- mantras and chanting, yoga, Tai chi, and doing arts and crafts. Once you find what works for you, you can begin each meditation by setting an intention.

Receiving Messages

Messages are never as loud and clear as you'd hope. Television makes them seem as if they arrive instantly and in complete sentences. Not so, for me anyway. I might receive phrases or words, but rarely full sentences. Information from Spirit is very subtle--little images and pieces, nudges and whispers that you will question. If you pay close attention and track the successes, you can discern which bits are worthy and how they arrive. With time and practice, you'll learn to trust the messages you receive.

Am I Meditating Correctly?

There's no correct way to relax your mind, only what works for you. Adding intention only means you have your antenna tuned to catch a specific frequency.

Before touch-screens, there were dials and nobs. Radio was "dialed in" to connect to a station. Meditation dials in the connection.

Where loved-ones are concerned, it takes a lot of energy for deceased spirits to communicate. Imagine that you are in a hot air balloon, rising to meet divine heights you have requested.

Intention

Fan the Flame

If meditation is the foundation of spiritual practice, intention is the power source. Setting an intention is not a passive wish but an active manifestation, a thought (or idea) that requires action to achieve your desired outcome. Before entering meditation, you might have the thought, "I will connect to the Divine for the answer to XYZ problem." That becomes your intention.

Know What You Want, and Why You Want It

The intention is the purpose -- what you want *plus* what you are willing to do to get it.

You can accomplish so much by working diligently with clear intention and finding ways to act. All accomplishments begin with intention.

Say you want to get a better job. Until you know exactly what sort of job you want, you cannot begin the search. If you look for "anything for a paycheck" that is what you will find. Same goes for a romantic partner. If you don't know what sort of person you are seeking, it's difficult to find them. Deciding what you want magnetizes you to attract those very things.

Most of us are overflowing with good intentions but fail to follow through with action. Your intention might be to get in better shape, but until you get moving, you won't get any more fit. Life isn't a fairy tale. We must actively live it, not wait for a wizard to grant wishes.

Our Intentions Aren't Always Best

Imagine that. We don't always know what is good for us!

How many relationships (friend, lover, or business partner) have you been in that ended with regret?

How many classes have you taken that didn't help you achieve your goals?

How many helpful tools have you purchased to banish to a box, garage, or closet?

How many bad books have you read or lousy movies have you seen?

All of those "wrong" choices seemed right at the time, based on your circumstances and data available. Faced with different circumstances and timing, you may have made different decisions. Or a wrong choice might have been what you needed to learn to make a better choice next time.

Every Experience is Valuable

Be grateful, especially for the hard stuff. If life was easy, you'd get bored and never learn anything new.

My original intention on my metaphysical path was to figure out what to do with the fragments of information that arrived like raindrops. *What am I supposed to do with this?* The practical side of me wanted useful information. I wanted to understand why unrelated bits arrived that made no sense. Was I damaged from a couple of concussions? Losing my marbles? A specimen for aliens?

Each meditation session, I set the intention. "Please show me what to do with the information I receive." Eventually, I shared with others of like-mind and wrote about some of the experiences in the novels *Warning Signs* and *Ursa Rising*. Then I set intentions for peace, healing, direction, but always for answers.

Divine Timing

I didn't always receive answers when I requested them. Emotional attachment to an outcome can create an obstacle to answers. If we try too hard, we can slow the flow.

Prayer

Many Ways to Pray

Prayer is a sensitive topic. For some, prayer can be the action portion of their practice. We might pray for everything from getting out of trouble to what we want for Christmas. We praise, confess, promise, atone, but mostly we make requests.

It doesn't matter who we pray to if we do it with reverence and gratitude. Then take action toward what we prayed about.

Anne Lamont wrote a book called *Help, Thanks, Wow*.

> When you need help, *Ask*.
> When you get what you asked for say, *Thanks*.
> When you don't need help and life treats you well, *Wow*.

Don't believe in prayer? Think good vibrations, positive thoughts, and good energy. Quantifiable studies have been done with plants, animals, food items, and sick people who recovered after being prayed over.

Ask to Receive

No matter how we ask, or who we ask, we must first ask to receive.

Placing conditions on exactly how we expect to receive will create walls that keep our thoughts and prayers from being answered.

Life Isn't Fair

. . . but it usually evens the odds down the road.

Say that you are owed money. Instead of specifying who, what, when, where, and how the money should return to you, pray for the amount owed to find its way back from any source.

Have Faith, Not Fear

Prayer is based in faith. If you are without faith, your prayers will be empty words. Trust that whatever you pray for will arrive as it chooses. If you fear that your prayers will go unanswered, you might as well spare yourself the effort because fear immediately places the request on hold.

John Edward's *Practical Praying* is from a Roman Catholic perspective.

Limitless, Not Limiting

Specifics are great, but not so many that they limit the possibilities. *Pray for what you want, not what you don't.* Use only positive words. Avoid the words Don't, Can't, Shouldn't, Couldn't, No, Not, Never.

"Help me find the path to the job aligned with my talents and skills."

> *Not:* "No more retail jobs."

"Help me grow into my ideal self so that I may attract my ideal partner."

> *Not:* "Make Joe Smith fall in love with me because he's my soulmate."

"Help me find ways to make the money I need to pay my obligations on time."

> *Not:* "Give me the numbers for the Powerball this week."

Praying for retribution or payback will only create a karmic debt that you will need to repay. Let karma take care of those who have wronged you. You may never see it come back around, but it will relieve you of the stress and harmful negative energy returning to you.

Get to Work

Without action, prayer is merely the hope of a dream. You can hope your life away without ever seeing tangible results. I knew a guy who hoped he would become wealthy by the time he was forty but had no clue as to how to achieve that.

He could pray for wealth until the end of time, but unless he had a plan of action, that desire would never come to fruition. And I don't believe anyone should pray for material wealth, but an abundance of healthy tools that help to build a great life. Money is awesome, but it isn't the only ingredient to happiness.

You can pray for a friend to find a job, but if they aren't actively looking--sending out resumes or making phone calls – the prayer will not gain traction.

Thoughts become things, so put only good things into your energy field and atmosphere. Like birds, you never know where they will land.

Thoughts and Words

Every Thought Feeds Your Energy

The thoughts that become influential are typically negative – trash that clutters your space.

You might think a million thoughts a day. Ask of each: Is this good, kind, or necessary? If not, discard it. Keep only the thoughts that work toward a positive outcome. It isn't until you take action that they become tangible.

Focus on the How Before the Why

Initially, don't waste energy on why you have a problem. Solve the problem. You can overthink a problem to death and still won't drill down to why. Will knowing why solve the problem?

Sometimes. Mechanics live by this, but people are more complex than cars. Some work with therapists for years trying to figure out the why.

Knowing why can be helpful in preventing the event from recurring. But spinning your wheels won't help you get unstuck. Many of us can't move forward until we have an answer. But our minds can rationalize answers *just to have an answer*. Doesn't make them true. I'd rather keep moving forward and figure out the why later.

Lost a job? Focus on finding another or more education.

Bad break-up? Focus on your growth.

Diagnosed with illness? Focus on the healing protocol.

Solve the problem before backtracking to assess why.

Mind Your Thoughts and Words

Your words create (or deflate) everything. Words are where we live. So if what we say creates ripples in the world, why not spread goodness? If negative or fearful thoughts come, you can rewrite them as lighter or positive ones.

This doesn't mean that you never have dark or negative thoughts. Your shadow side needs expression. But you do have control over what you unleash into the world. Take care. Think before you speak. Once hurtful words go out there, there is no getting them back. Apologizing with "I didn't mean it" rings hollow. You did mean it in the heat of the moment. Guard your thoughts and words like buried treasure. They are the currency of creation.

Purpose

"What is my purpose?"

You probably hope to hear something like, "You will become a scientist and be part of the team that cures cancer."

Your purpose isn't necessarily what you do, but how you integrate yourself into what you are doing with intention. No one should be telling you what to do or who you should become in life. You have free will to make your own choices. Experience life through your unique perspective. Make the best of yourself with your talents to create the way of life that matters to you then share it with others.

Live Like You Matter

. . . with as much grace as possible. That's everyone's purpose. What matters to you today, may not tomorrow. You have the right to change direction. Remember that every thought, decision, and action ripples outward affecting everyone in your sphere of influence.

Purpose is what you do to bring value to your little corner of the world. That may not necessarily be what pays the bills. It is where your choices and your creations contribute to change in yourself, your environment, and others who inhabit it. Doing things important to you have a ripple effect. For me, art, spiritual endeavors, nature and wildlife matter. For you, it might be science, technology, commerce, children, and legacy.

What Matters to You?

What brings you true joy? Where do your interests and creations connect? Having a love of food doesn't mean you must open a restaurant or be a farmer. You might become the best cook in the family or the local soup kitchen.

Serving your purpose means doing *what matters to you* while you are having a human experience. If it matters to you, it matters to someone else. Perhaps it's important to you to insight change or right injustice. What would you like to see change? What would you like to make matter? Be that. Do that. Connect with others of like-mind.

It doesn't matter if you are a waiter, trash collector, district attorney or neurosurgeon. Do your very best at whatever you choose, wherever you are in this moment.

I think a better question is: How can I best serve (the world or others)? And in what capacity?

You will serve many purposes throughout your lifetime. Instead of chasing one vocation or occupation, learn to be your best, right here and now, by living like you matter and capitalizing on your uniqueness. Add the ingredient of yourself to whatever you do, then share it with others.

Adam Leipzig gave a TEDx talk on how to find your life purpose by answering these questions:

1. Who am I? (Your name)
2. What do I do naturally, effortlessly? (what you enjoy)
3. Who do I do it for?
4. What do others want and need?
5. How do others change because of my doing what I do best?

How to Find Your Life Purpose in 5 Minutes is actually ten minutes long, but time well spent:

https://www.youtube.com/watch?v=vVsXO9brK7M

Others will try to place you into a neatly wrapped package, but it's up to you to show the world what is deep inside.

Tools

Choose a Tool

Tools are items of focus to help awaken your abilities. What attracts you?

Astrology	Tarot/Oracle cards
Pendulum, dowsing	Numerology
Spirit boards	Runes/Bones
I-Ching	Palmistry
Tea Leaves	Crystals
Mediumship	Scrying or gazing
Herbs, essential oils	Reiki, touch healing
Hypnosis, Dreams	Shamanism
Earth Magic	Handwriting Analysis
Prayer, affirmation	Akashic records
Automatic Writing	Psychometry
Art	Astral Travel

When I was a kid, I was a rock hound. Still am. A dollar used to get me five tumbled stones from a local flea market vendor. It took me a long time to pick them out. I didn't know they were crystals with metaphysical properties. I just liked them. Then I learned that every stone emits a vibration or energy that helps to enhance certain qualities or abilities in us.

Use Your Tools

Carrying a computer around won't do a thing for you unless you learn to use it. As with any tool, you must use it often and make it a part of your life.

A tennis player uses a racquet, but without training on how to wield it, fitness and nutritional regimen, psychological conditioning for the mental game, and years of consistent practice, that racquet is nothing more than a decoration. The one hanging in my garage won't make me a better player.

Make Your Tools Uniquely Yours

All tools have great things to offer depending on perspective and the knowledge implemented. Layers and layers of meaning build with time.

Bring your unique skills and strengths to your tools. If you analyze where you excel, you'll be able to use that energy or vibration to work with the tool. Tools can be used to help with things like love, career, health, and spiritual connection. But you may come up with something new and invent a whole different technique. But you need to use it or lose it.

Practice Fuels Consistency

Practice your tools as if you plan to turn professional with them. You didn't learn to draw, cook, or sing on key the first time you tried. Skill development takes repetition. Give any tool an honest go. I bought my first tarot deck back in the 80s. (No, you don't have to be gifted your first deck.) I was so disturbed by the depressing medieval meanings in the enclosed leaflet, I tossed it into a drawer for ten years. Eventually, I discovered tarot was a tool that could grow with you throughout a lifetime of study. It's truly timeless.

You might be drawn to combine more than one tool. I often use a pendulum and numerology with the tarot. Others might use astrology and tarot together. Do what works for you in your own way.

In the 80s, astrology took a bashing when First Lady Nancy Reagan consulted an astrologer in the White House. Astrologers used to be the gurus that kings and emperors relied on for all political decisions. Prophets like Nostradamus leaned heavily on astrology because it was right there in the sky.

In the past, advisers had been so accurate in their predictions that they were executed or imprisoned for fear of becoming more powerful than their leaders. The accuracy is what makes it scary. Don't knock it until you've tried it.

65

Ritual

Prepare, Perform, Repeat

Ritual is the proper preparation for performing a task or ceremony.

When you first learn to drive, you have a ritual: adjust the seat, buckle your seat belt, position the mirrors, key in the ignition, say a little prayer, check your mirrors again. After you get your license and drive regularly, it becomes a muscle memory so that your body takes over that part of the work, freeing your mind for other thoughts.

The same goes for psychic development.

You can begin a meditation ritual with smudging, music, candles, and setting an intention. Over time, a ritual can make things happen on auto-pilot.

And when you leave something out of your ritual, you might feel a void. Imagine forgetting to brush your teeth. You feel as if everything will go sideways until you go back and do it. The more you practice, the more the habit sticks.

Doing your work at the same time every day helps establish a ritual. It programs your subconscious mind with expectation. In today's supersonic world, flexibility is key. You can change your ritual as you grow -- lengthen or shorten, add or remove elements.

How Do I Develop a Ritual?

Schedule the time! Start with 5 or 10 minutes for 21 days. Once that sticks, you can increase the time. Putting your meditation or spiritual ritual time on the calendar or to-do list may be the only way it won't get shoved to the bottom of your priorities.

Routine vs. Ritual

Routine is a detailed course of action that becomes a habit. Reading the paper with coffee in the morning, having a workout, and daily meditation time are examples of a routine. Ritual is ordered for a specific purpose. Rituals might include setting up an altar, dressing a candle, doing meditation, spell casting, or performing a holiday rite. For Catholics, Mass is a ritual. Jews fast on the Sabbath. Pagans perform magical workings according to season.

What Do I Need?

That depends on what you wish to accomplish. Whatever you choose: prayer, incantations, meditation, yoga, altar building, intention, healing energy, tools, study guides, etc.

When I prepare to read the tarot, I have a ritual to establish the boundaries and create sacred space along with personal protection. Then I request clear spiritual communication guide me toward the client's best interests, success, and growth. Not necessarily what they want to hear.

After you've made an intentional connection and acted on it, you can achieve creation.

Accountability

It's On You

You are the star of your own story. In your movie, you are the lead, and it's up to you to set the stage to find solutions to your problems. Even if you didn't cause the disturbance or chaos, account for your participation. You can remove yourself from situations or change your responses to whatever occurs. Don't look to others for the root of the problem. You are front and center. The nucleus. The hub. You have the power to change the energy around you or exit the scene for higher ground.

"You don't know me or my life!"

I don't have to. I know my own. When my environment is problematic (or chaotic), I ask myself, "What about the problem, person, or situation *is me*?" It can be quite a revelation, but you must be honest with yourself. What you see happening in your environment reflects what is going on inside you. If you've got chaos orbiting around you, something inside you is attracting that. If you can't see anything resembling yourself in the energy, then allow it to be a window into

69

what you do not want, so you can change your course.

You become a magnet for whatever energy circles you. Take care. Life can send you exactly what you ask for. When we are seeking to escape or balance, the "opposites attract" rule comes into play.

Things in Your Control

Your attitude, your decisions, your moods, your behavior, and your words are under your control. You can change your external environment and some of the chaos in it. Own your choices. You can choose to limit exposure to people and situations that don't support you or bring positive energy to your life. You can leave a dead-end job with the impossible-to-please boss or back away from friends who are overly critical. If you chose to do nothing, you'll continue to attract more of the same.

Own the Energy You Carry

You alone are responsible for any energy you create, conjure, and release into the world :your lousy mood, your readings for others, and magical workings, etc.. Energies or entities that you conjure will come back around, so be ready. As an adult, you make choices. If you get into a jam, it's up to you to get yourself out.

If you don't know how to manage and return unwanted energy or entities, don't request an appearance. Those who have dabbled after watching movies or reading select sections of books think they can go about their lives when they are done playing. Sorry, but if you open the window, don't complain about the bugs that come in. You will be held accountable.

Account for every step in your process so that you can do damage control. You are responsible for every action you take, every decision you make, and every word you say. Because in the end, it's all on you no matter who else is involved.

One weak, unprotected moment – to see what might happen -- can change your life.

Need a few clichés?

> You play, you pay.

> You're an adult, act like it.

> You made your bed, now lie in it.

Dr. Wayne Dyer's book *There's a Spiritual Solution to Every Problem* covers accountability in connection to source.

Doubt and Discernment

Have doubts?

Trust in Something Greater Than Yourself

There is an unseen energy that connects us to a divine source. Believe in your ability to plug into that. Trust develops with practice, seeking teachers, reading and experimentation. In short, doing the work.

Fear Rules Doubt

What you think can manifest. When you create fear, you can either grow it or destroy it. The easiest way to destroy fear is to expose it or desensitize it. Do what you can to face your fears before they become lifetime companions.

How do you learn to trust the information you receive?

Validation and Consistency

I never doubt the synchronicity of the forces of the Universe. But on occasion, I doubt my clarity and interpretations. We are all connected to the Universal source and it can take time to fully trust that connection.

Consistent practice builds confidence and lessens doubt. Validate as much as you can, either from whom you are reading or research. Signs appear everywhere if you have eyes to see them. Numbers, words and phrases, sounds, music, imagery, even nature can point you in a direction or offer a mirror of reflection. If you develop into a living oracle, you'll see patterns and answers in everything from cloud formations to cat litter.

If you have a like-minded friend with which to do spiritual work, you can double the energy and validate each other's insights. Often, you'll receive the same information and create a bridge with regular practice. It is quite exciting to finish each other's interpretations.

Patience, Practice, and Persistence Pay

Your patience will be tested. There will be times when you have orchestrated the perfect meditation time and space only to receive nothing but silence. Other times you may have no expectations and receive a tidal wave of unexpected details.

Expectation can be an obstacle. To keep the river of spiritual connection of data flowing, let go of any preconceived notions. Otherwise, those thoughts and desires pile into a log-jam. Let go of what you think you need and be open to what comes. It's probably exactly what you need at that moment. In my opening story, I didn't get what I expected from the psychic, but I did get what I needed.

Doubt is Natural

Doubt is the shadow side of confidence and we must work through it. You won't be able to eliminate doubt completely. No one fully trusts every piece of information they receive, nor do they instantly understand the context. Human beings are imperfect creatures. And perception is specific to the individual. Being skeptical keeps you searching and validating.

Faith Over Fear

In psychic development, you have two choices when doubt arrives. 1. Have faith and trust the information, or 2. Freeze in fear. You decide how to function, with faith or with fear.

"You're the psychic. You tell me."

Being psychic doesn't mean you will have all the answers or know every detail about anyone. You won't be able to read anyone's mind, although some claim they can. You will receive pieces of data with which to connect the dots.

Imagine that every person or situation is a thousand-piece puzzle. Your intuition might pick up a piece of a corner, a piece of the foundation, or a piece of the center. Without all the pieces, it's hard to form a complete picture. And the Universe rarely provides information that is truly none of our business: Social Security numbers, bank accounts, credit card numbers, or other proprietary information. I've only heard of one psychic in the world that was truly gifted with numbers. The deepest, darkest secrets won't come out unless the individual is ready to do the work and face the emotions attached to them. Your psychic knows what you already know but might be denying.

Discernment

Sometimes you get an impression of the energy around the person's emotions or an area of their life that needs attention. But is that person ready to hear that information? Because it's not always pleasant. Trust your instincts. Delivering bad news is never fun and requires diplomacy. You don't want to make an already difficult situation worse or plant a seed that creates a self-fulfilled prophecy. The news may be bad but withholding it could be even worse. Trust your intuition to *feel* what is best for all involved.

The best article I've ever read on discernment is at https://lonerwolf.com/spiritual-discernment/

It's Not About You

As your skills grow, you'll need to be careful not to get caught up in ego and forget that you are a small part of a much larger landscape. You bring a unique blend of energy, aptitude, and perspective to the table. Most importantly, in psychic work, it's never about you.

Sure, in early development, it's all about you--your purpose, your career, your health, and well-being. If you seek to become a professional in the metaphysical field, it becomes all about the people you serve. When your clients sing your praises and boost your ego, remember that it was not you but the spiritual team behind you. You are the only receiver.

Trust What You Feel Over What You Think

If you feel in your gut that the information is untrustworthy, trust that. It is your right to accept or reject any ideas as only you are responsible for the choices you make because of them.

Always go with your first impression. It comes from the heart (subconscious "feeling" mind). Intellect can interfere because it comes from the head (conscious "thinking" mind). Your head can talk the heart out of anything, like a protective parent.

Question any information that creates fear. Fear stops motion. Fear of judgment, fear of failure or success, fear of criticism, fear of looking stupid. The list is endless. Whatever is born of fear should be re-examined in faith.

The Truth Comes Out

Telling the truth gets right down to business and forces you to face the problem head-on so you can work through the obstacles. Becoming a lawyer to please your parents when you'd rather play music will only come back to haunt you. You will obsess over the what-ifs and what-might-have-beens. Most regrets come from things we don't do.

I met a woman who was miserable in her work. I could see that she was better suited working in the field she had previously--a job she had loved. When I asked why she'd let go of something she enjoyed for a job that she didn't, she looked away. "Money. Expectation."

Her family and friends had talked her into getting a "real job."

"How's that going?"

She shook her head looking almost ashamed to admit that she missed her old job. In the end, she was relieved to hear that doing what she loved was nothing to be ashamed of. Some of us are a perfect fit for unpopular positions.

Life is Not One-Size-Fits-All

If it feels right and makes you happy, it is your truth. Living your truth may require some courage, patience, and juggling. Life can be expensive.

You might have to make sacrifices to save the money for the education or tools needed to achieve your goals. If you're an independent adult who pays your way to support your endeavors, what are you waiting for? Have the courage to become who you want. It's your life. It is when you are beholden to others for financial support that boundaries blur. If someone else is paying for the roof over your head and other necessities while you're "blowing your tiny paycheck on your hobby," you'll have an uphill battle on your hands.

Have a family? Imagine that your children witness how miserable you are in your day job and never see you pursue a dream. Will they follow your example?

You will have doubts about where your chosen path may lead, whether it will be worth the time, money, and sacrifice. Make choices (and plans) on where to spend your resources and energy.

Small steps every day can keep you focused while helping heal some of the stress from your day job.

Repay Your Debts

Be responsible enough to repay your debt to whoever helps you start out. Work the lousy day job for a while so that you aren't placing a heavy burden on your benefactors or maxing out your credit cards. There are times that you must do things you don't enjoy, but not for the rest of your life. And you can learn so much from undesirable jobs – money management, business skills, communication, technology, emotional intelligence, and patience. Having a variety of skills affords you the freedom and versatility to create the life you want.

Get Out of Your Comfort Zone

To grow in any area, you must leave the safety of your comfort zone. Get out of your nest and try things that scare you. Risks offer no guarantees, but fear and doubt ensure that you will never chase any dream. Give it a go.

Objectivity

If you stand close to an impressionist painting, you'll see colors, shapes, brushstrokes, and imperfections. Take a few steps back, and it becomes clear. In some cases, as clear as a photograph. The same can be said for self. You are too close to see yourself, so it is wise to let someone neutral take an objective look at you now and then. Someone who has no emotional investment in you. Friends and family will choose to spare your feelings over being honest.

No One Has All the Answers

If you think you do, slap yourself with a reality check. No matter how educated, practiced, or certified you are, you will not have answers to every question. You may even receive conflicting data. You will question your abilities, your accuracy, and interpretations. In psychic development, there is no finish line, and no point of arrival, no pot of gold, and no end. Information from the cosmos is infinite, whether you believe there is anything "out there" or that it all comes from inside, the well never runs dry.

Pagans, Wiccans, Native Americans and other indigenous people work with nature because it is a perfect system. Human creations are not. Knowledge is infinite. Energy is infinite. As a singular individual, you can't know everything. But with discernment, you have access to the information you need.

Truth is Not Universal

I wish I could tell you that everything I say here is the absolute truth for everyone. If there is one thing I know for sure, truth is as individual as fingerprints.

Your truth filters through the lens of your belief system and experiences. Siblings who grow up in the same household can have completely different truths based on their perspective.

Interpretation

When you read a book or see a film, you'll come away with something different than the person next to you because you viewed the story through a different lens. Your interpretation is your truth from your point of view, your will, your memories, reference points, culture, upbringing, even bias.

Not every psychic reader can connect with every person. When you see a reader, know that their truth or interpretation may not be aligned with yours. Yours might be more literal when the reader's might be more metaphoric. How the information comes through might not make sense at that moment, but it might make perfect sense later. Clients can be quick to dismiss a reading that didn't give them every detail they expected. No psychic can control what comes through. It either comes, or it doesn't. That is why recording is so important. References might not make sense until a few days later, then bang! It dawns on you. And if it does, let the reader know. It helps them trust the impressions they receive.

Truth is specific to each of us. That's why you don't like meatloaf, beards, Calypso music, or algebra. Or why you love lavender, toads, soft cheese, and gray hair. Or why you hate injustice, fear old barns, or adore the bagpipes. Those sorts of details become your truth.

Recording Your Progress

Record Everything

Whether you are recording your own psychic impressions or a professional reading, having all the details will go a long way to tracking your growth and recurring patterns as you move toward proficiency.

> I prefer the word proficiency to mastery. No matter how much we discover, there will always be more to learn. The Universe holds an endless supply of secrets. If you do reach a certain level of skill, keep your ego in check. What the Universe gives, it can take away.

Memory is not as reliable as we'd like to believe. Ask any criminal attorney. Little things can and will slip through the cracks. You will forget details that might be key to unlocking a crucial message from your dreams, intuitive hits, meditations, and any other moments of significance. Some details might not make sense when you receive them, so it's important to compile them for later assessment. And a little distance can do wonders for clarity. It will also give you a catalogue of symbology to reference.

I have notebooks full of nonsensical words, imagery and ideas. The majority might seem insignificant, but there might be jewels that make perfect sense later.

Record it all: numbers, colors, people, feelings, emotions, impressions, sounds, smells, tastes, weather, and time. You never know what might be relevant. You'll be able to put patterns together for progress.

Letting Go

Clean Out Your Mental Closet

From outdated beliefs to negative thinking, if it doesn't help, it hinders. Let go of anything that doesn't work *for you*.

Re-leasing is a renewal of the very ideas and old stuff that you seek to eliminate. Like re-leasing your apartment for another year.

Herman Siu said, "Learn to let go. The past has nothing new to say."

Letting go cleanses and removes mental and emotional obstacles. In a negative situation, letting go of old energy creates space for good works. Anger and frustration need to be let out like steam from a boiling pot.

Meditate to Let Go

Get still, inhale positivity (plus signs) then exhale negativity (minus signs) in a strong whoosh to disburse energy. Imagine drawing in good and letting bad go.

Use a visual meditation

1. See yourself handing your troubles to the Universe or to a trusted energy or deity.

2. Let problems go into the setting sun. *Be careful that you don't recollect them after letting go*. Move on.

3. Visualize pulling petals from a flower, each representing a worry or problem that you haven't been able to solve. Toss them into a stream and watch the water carry them away.

4. Prefer animals? Do a meditation with your animal spirit. What creature appears? Research the qualities and behaviors of the animal. Allow the animal to take any issues with it when it leaves.

Only 20% of us are visual. If you can't "see," utilize one of your other senses. In any manner that you "imagine."

5. Let go in the Violet Flame.

What is the Violet Flame? Exactly what it sounds like. Elizabeth Claire Prophet's *Violet Flame to Heal Body, Mind, and Soul* (recently re-issued) speaks of its ability to heal the physical, mental, emotional and spiritual bodies. It burns off all negative energy as an earthly fire would burn a marshmallow to ash. You meld into the Violet Flame itself, allowing it to envelop you and enter your being.

Gratitude

A grateful heart is a peaceful heart. Being grateful pays forward positivity and lightness of being. It keeps your psychic door open and the river of reception flowing as well has having physiological benefits.

Be grateful for everything in your life, even the hard stuff.

You can keep journals dedicated to gratitude but saying a sincere "Thank You" is quick and easy. No time or ritual required.

Straight from the heart. Thank you!

That is all.

The Dark Side

Light in the Dark

"But I don't deal with anything dark."

You may not choose to engage the Dark Side, but in a world of duality, you can't avoid it completely. Don't think you can do spiritual work without occasional brushes with darkness, if only from other people. Knowledge is power. Best not to bury your head in the sand. The more you know, the more you can protect yourself.

Shining your light makes you as visible to dark energies as social media does on the web. If you understand that the Universe has duality and requires balance, you can respect the role the dark side plays.

Our world already has an abundance of darkness. Without light, there would be no shadow and vice versa. And, as much as we'd like to deny it, we all have a shadow side. Emotions like anger, envy, and jealousy live in all of us. But what about energies outside our personalities?

Be Aware, Not Scared

Unseen dark energies count on naïve, distracted, or easy targets like drug and alcohol abusers, over-medicated, and depressed folks. Lower energies feed off our negativity. Substance impairment makes using divination tools potentially hazardous if you ask or demand a response. Don't drink and divine.

Because energies can also use your opposing light energy to recharge, you can be a perfectly healthy light being and still be targeted. They can drain your battery, and even neutralize you as a threat. Psychic protection is critical.

Don't Disrespect the Dark

Flat out, don't be the dabbler who conjures a lower energy "just to see" then doesn't know how to return it to the Other World. How would you like being summoned to the boss's office to sit there ignored? Don't think that because these energies are heavier that they don't deserve respect. They have a purpose in the spiritual ecosystem.

People can abuse the Light Side and claim to be more evolved than they are. Spirit deserves all the credit. You are only a pathway.

Discerning the Dark

Dark energies are skilled at disguising themselves as friends, guides, and loved ones. If the messages you receive are abusive or negative, harmful to yourself or others, they have dark intent. If they make you feel bad about yourself, or your decisions, if they tear you down, deflate your self-worth, or encourage further pain, they are dark. Do not engage or limit your exposure to the negative ones. After all, you can't un-hear or un-see the undesirable.

As with any mutual relationship, you agree to an exchange of some kind. Darker energies live to take. Once you make the connection, they stick like Velcro. And if they grant your request, there will be a price to be paid.

What feeds darkness?

The Negativity Loop

You know that tape that replays all your negative hits on your mental turntable? That is mental programming. Negative thoughts stick. Positive thoughts often end up in the trash bin because they don't feel as trustworthy. We are hit with an avalanche of negativity on daily basis from media outlets, work, family, and ourselves. If you get stuck with the negative tape looping in your mind, STOP! Change your state of mind by rewriting your negativity into productivity. Create something. Move! Exercise oxygenates the blood which lifts your spirits naturally. Reach for some comedy, enjoy nature, play with children or pets.

Isolation and Ignoring Signs

We can see others so clearly because they are at a distance. Riding around in our skin, we can't get enough objectivity. Often, we feel lost, stuck in a rut. Isolated and exhausted, our minds make things worse than they are. Friends and family do their best to offer advice that may fall short of being helpful. This is when we should seek professional advice. Conventional or unconventional, find someone who can offer a fresh perspective from an angle that you might not have considered. You know the truth, but fear admitting it or won't face it until someone holds up a mirror of perspective. We aren't always honest with ourselves. Improvement is work. And our lives are already challenging. Still, it falls on you to not remain isolated.

Awareness

If you've dabbled in any dark art, you are "on the grid" or "on the radar." Used a spirit board as a game instead of a tool without reverence and respect? You lit up on the grid. Attended a séance for Halloween fun? You lit up on the grid. Performed a ritual in any half-hearted manner or didn't close the door you opened? You lit up on the grid.

As soon as you make that connection, you can be noticed as if you've activated a cell phone.

Be Reverent and Respectful

Instead of fear, I choose to have the same healthy respect for the dark as I would a coiled snake. Since I'm not familiar with many species of snake, I treat them all as dangerous. No sudden movements. *You don't bother me, and I won't bother you. If you try to hurt me, I will defend myself.*

Don't Feed the Fear

Many dark energies are dead folks who were miserable and nasty in life. Enlightenment doesn't necessarily find them in death. I disengage from those energies as I do with the verbally abusive and bullying. Non-human energies siphon light. That's their job. The dark ones *need* you to fear them to have power over you. Their intent is control. Like any bully, they hate to be exposed. As soon as light shines on them, most dissolve back into the darkness or move on to easier targets. But there are exceptions.

Dark things come in many varieties of crafty and cunning, bumbling and badgering. Even if they're tired, don't assume that you are smarter or quicker than they are. Have your protection in place when dealing with any supernatural energy. Luck favors the prepared.

Be Careful Who or What You Ask For

A surefire way to pick a fight is to demand a response. "Show us you are here." You might as well poke a Hell's Angel in the chest with a ball bat. If you command that they prove themselves, or (even dumber) provoke them to make physical contact, who do you think will muscle their way to you? The bad apples. And we don't know enough about the non-human ones. Some are powerful enough to cause harm. Ghost hunting TV shows often say that "ghosts can't hurt you." Most of them won't, but we aren't talking about deceased loved ones here. Be careful who you invite to the party.

How would you like a stranger to barge into your house and *demand* that you entertain them? You opened the door inviting them in, then you got mad because they wouldn't leave.

Every relationship has a level of reciprocity; if you invite them to the party, you will be expected to offer something in return. And if you call it, it's your responsibility to send it back.

Frequently Asked Questions

How do I know that the information I receive isn't coming from my imagination?

Society has conditioned us to believe that imagination isn't real. But imagination is what brought our new technology to fruition. Imagination is creativity, thoughts that manifest into form. Your imagination is your asset. It is the space where Spirit co-creates.

Learn to trust information by finding ways to validate what you receive. Your human nature will have doubts. If we didn't doubt, we wouldn't dig deeper. You may not find immediate answers, but the search could lead you to other useful tidbits.

Once I'm proficient in my psychic abilities, will I be able to read anyone?

Many practitioners will say they can read anyone, fearing how the world perceives them. But no. Ethically, you should only read people with their permission. There will also be circumstances where your guides won't allow you to connect with someone. Respect that. And then there are people you won't be able to connect to because of their own fear or bias. You may not be the person they will listen to. Don't take this personally.

Some people will unconsciously build energetic boundaries because they don't wish to be read. Natural psychic protection! It is their free will to protect themselves from anything they fear or mistrust. (If they are trying a psychic reading for the first time, it might be to make a friend happy or to prove the reader wrong.)

You shouldn't read people closest to you. They are meant to be teachers, healers, and leaders in your life.

We all need safety and trust in our relationships. I don't feel that I should read my husband. I don't believe that everything about him is for me to know. Together, we can have a more authentic marriage if I can't peek into his private stuff. We also need to respect each other's personal space.

Always get permission to read someone, or deal with the karma of being a psychic spy.

If you're so psychic, why don't you always make the right decisions in your life?

Like you, I'm living an authentic human experience. I can't get far enough away from myself for true objectivity. If I have my nose pressed against a mirror, I can't see much more than my face. No one has all the answers. No matter what their level of achievement.

"You tell me. You're the psychic."

And so are you. But neither of us are mind-readers, are we? I'm not allowed to be inside your head. I don't know what you are thinking, what you want to eat, who you have a crush on, or details of all your dirty little secrets. I'm not allowed to see things that are proprietary like ID numbers. If you want details, be more open to my entering this space with you.

Couples feel that after they've been with their partners for a while, "They should know (what I want, need, desire, or require)." We need to communicate what we want and not assume that someone we love *just knows*, even if they are psychic.

As a client, you have a role in the reading. Even though you don't wish to communicate many details before your session, you can help by granting your guides and spirit helper's permission to communicate with the reader's spiritual team. Not speaking or even nodding for fear of revealing something doesn't help you get the most of your time or money.

Don't ask, "How is my life going to go?" or "Will I be successful?" Those are questions only you will have the answers to based on the choices you make every day. If you are willing to do the work toward goals that bring you joy and satisfaction, then you're on a path that is right for you.

Want a great reading? Be willing to validate information, be open to dialogue without being too revealing, and ask the questions you *really* want answers to.

Why should I see a psychic if they aren't going to tell me what to do?

Primarily, to validate what you intuitively know, but don't fully trust. It is quite powerful to have someone who doesn't know you from a lamp post confirm your suspicions, expand your perspective, or shine a light on an area that needs attention. Objectivity makes all the difference.

When you are in crisis, you may think that you want a psychic to tell you what to do. You really don't. Only you truly know what is best for you. Allow yourself discovery time. And if you still want someone to make your decisions for you, remind yourself that you have the gift of choice when many do not.

Trust that intuitive "pull" you may feel toward or away from something. Ask your psychic clear questions to look specifically at both sides of a problem so that you can make an informed decision.

Do I need to have a Near Death Experience to be strongly psychic?

Some big names in the psychic world come with stories of awakening from an NDE, but we are all born with a level of psychic aptitude. Some are born wide awake and others need to work at it. Traumatic experiences can shock the psychic door open, so to speak.

What is the difference between prayer and incantation?

Prayer is a religious request or petition to a deity with the hope of a specific outcome.

Incantation is a command or statement issued in ritual magic on how it will be, often done in rhyme. So, it is.

What is the difference between experimenting and dabbling?

Experimenting is sampling with the intention of practicing long enough to determine value, completing the project or class, before moving onto the next.

Dabbling is when you try something you know little about, then abandon it before you receive a result. Resist "shiny object syndrome" and stick with a tool until you feel you've achieved a strong level of proficiency.

I strongly caution against dabbling. It will only get you into trouble. If you see something that interests you, research it thoroughly and ask questions of an expert before dipping your toe in any modality.

Remember, Hollywood is not an expert in the supernatural. It's not an entertainer's responsibility to educate. Psychics on television may employ precautions that get cut from the show because they are considered dull, time-consuming, or proprietary.

As a medium, can I talk to my deceased relatives whenever I want?

Short answer? You can, but you shouldn't.

There are a lot of ethical factors to consider. How long the person has been in the Other World, the circumstances of their death, their personality, their religious beliefs, your relationship with them, their mental state, your need or intention for such constant communication.

Your loved one's spirit is not hanging around for your entertainment. Even though they no longer have physical responsibilities like a job, bills, or chores that doesn't mean they have nothing better to do. When a loved one dies, their spirit might linger through the grieving process to comfort the remaining family members. It is their free will to do so. Requesting that someone stick around for your selfish reasons only tethers that soul to the Living World. The longer they spend here without their body, the more heavily earthbound they can become.

Souls need to move forward in life and death. Be strong enough to allow your loved ones to leave so that they may continue their soul's journey, while you do your best to continue yours parted from them. You will only grow from understanding that you are part of the Living World and they are now part of the Other World.

> Cautionary tale: I met a young medium who regularly conversed with the spirit of a dear friend who had taken his own life. I urged her to let him go so he could move on and heal. The longer he lingered, the farther his energy grew from being the beloved friend she remembered. Her regular requests for him to communicate kept him tethered to a world he no longer belonged in. And he was growing dark.

After I encouraged her to stop communications for both their sakes, he threatened me. He was a troubled soul in life and had become more troubled in death.

What kinds of readings are there and what are the differences?

Cards or other tools: The reader connects to a querent's energy by using a physical tool such as cards, runes, stones, photos or objects provided by the querent. Astrology is in a class by itself, but a tool nonetheless.

Intuitive or channeling: The reader connects with the querent's energy without the use of physical tools.

Many folks think that if a reader doesn't need to use a tool, they are better or more psychic. I have not found this to be true. No reader has been able to connect with me without using a tool. I've been told that I'm a "tough read" by more than a couple, so I no longer try new intuitives. But that's me. I know people who swear by their intuitive reader, so you may have a completely opposite experience.

I have greater success with readers who uses tools as I do. You can dig a hole in the ground by using your bare hands, but it's far more efficient to use a shovel. You can go deeper and faster with the help of a tool.

Predictive vs. Choice-Based Styles: Some readers deliver information in a *predictive* style, which is to what is referred to as fortune-telling. It tells the querent what is may come to pass or how things may turn out. I prefer readings in a *choice-based* style that offers options for consideration so the querent can act to change their outcome of their own free will. For me, this style creates an informed individual who uses the knowledge to their own advantage.

Depending on your belief system, you will accept and manifest the prediction or take steps to change undesirable outcomes. I feel that a choice-based approach leaves the power in the hands of the querent where it belongs.

What are negative entities capable of?

Some are quite evolved and capable of interacting with the living. Spirits can start chattering at you constantly, not letting you sleep, twisting your dreams, physically touching you – leaving scratches or bruises. Severe cases have reported people being shoved, kicked, bitten, even sexually assaulted.

Worst case? Lower energies can latch on like ticks and have the advantage of being invisible to close-minded folks. Strong ones can step into your body and compromise your physical health. People who dabble with the Other World can open themselves up to contract illnesses that leave medical professionals scratching their heads. (They won't respond to medications as they should.) Extreme cases have reported perfectly healthy people having heart attacks, strokes, and other critical conditions. Cases like those often involve a burial ground near the property or dark magical practices that opened a door. Cases requiring exorcism are rare and should only be performed by an experienced authority of unyielding faith.

What is the difference between a spirit and a poltergeist?

A spirit is a supernatural energy from human to angel. It is the consciousness with contacts the former human personality. Spirit is the breath of life in us all.

A poltergeist or PK manifestation is a noisy, mischievous energy that likes to create physical disturbances. These are usually created by a living person with unmanaged psychic abilities.

Reminders and Parting Thoughts

Developing Your Intuition is Not All Fun and Games

As humans, we might be intelligent, but we are also emotionally impaired. Our best hope is to get out of our own way and utilize the resources we have, like our intuition.

Information you intuit may not always be rosy. You may see scary things involving loved-ones and good people. Some you might be powerless to change, but the people concerned might. Deliver "heads-up" knowledge with caution.

Be Willing to Make Mistakes

We can make our opportunities without limiting ourselves to anyone else's parameters. We can explore, be willing to test new ground and make lots of mistakes while utilizing any tools of protection available to you.

In readings, be willing to be wrong. No reader is 100% accurate all the time.

Do Your Due Diligence

Learn all you can before you attempt to engage with things you know little to nothing about. Don't know if it's friend or foe? Don't poke it with a stick.

Mind Your Words

Words can be weapons. In an emotionally charged moment, words go "out there," and there's no reeling them back in. Think before you speak. Words can cause more pain than knives because they are never forgotten. It's not always what you say, but how you say it.

Be Respectful to Everyone

Choosing the spiritual path requires integrity. Have the same respect for the Other World as you do your own. None of us know the full ramifications of these encounters. Explore as an academic for insight into what might be beyond this world. Have respect. No one has all the answers. It's not our world. We are only allowed glimpses.

Check Your Ego

Use tools with the proper intention. Even masters don't have all the answers. Yes, we still must try things to learn, and not be afraid to explore, but don't be afraid to ask questions of experts. Use psychic protection and common sense without going against your moral and ethical nature. Be smart.

Most Fear is a Waste of Energy

Particularly the fear of death. We all meet it. Need motivation? Allow time to propel you forward. You are on the clock from the moment you draw your first breath. You have a limited time in which to reach your potential, achieve your goals, create value, imprint your energy and leave a legacy in your small corner of the world. Spend your time on things that matter instead of dwelling on limitations. Focus on what you want, not what you don't.

Learn to say "No"

We don't have to say "yes" to everything, especially things we don't enjoy. Learning to say "no" can be soul-saving. When we do things for others purely out of obligation, no one benefits. As we age, we might feel taken for granted or used because we've generously said "yes" to everything then felt unappreciated and resentful when people don't seem to notice the effort we've expended and expected even more of us.

Self-Care

We must care for ourselves as well as we care for others. If we spend all our time pleasing others, there won't be anything left in our well. Selfish? Consider it self-preservation. The more we respect our time, energy, and spirit, the more others will learn to do the same. Self-respect is essential for our personal growth and development. Put yourself on top of the list.

At this writing, there is an epidemic of substance abuse in the U.S. as we self-medicate with alcohol, food, prescription and recreational drugs. We numb ourselves instead of dealing with the root of our problems. Pain is a part of life. Avoiding it is a waste of energy and resources. Long-term, it is better to face the pain head-on than try to avoid the feeling. Like ripping off a Band-Aid, you know it will hurt, but you get the pain over with. Seek professional help if necessary.

Respect your spirit, that 21 grams that chose your body as a vehicle to navigate this life. It is pure magnificent light and brilliance.

Suggested Reading and Resources

I curated this list based on personal experience. If your favorite category or personality is not listed, I have yet to explore them thoroughly enough to offer recommendations.

Biographies

George Anderson

We Don't Die

www.georgeanderson.com

Diane Brandon

Born Aware

www.dianebrandon.com

Chip Coffey

Growing Up Psychic

www.chipcoffey.com

John Edward

One Last Time

www.johnedward.net

Tyler Henry

Between Two Worlds: Lessons from the Other Side

www.tylerhenryhollywoodmedium.com

John Holland

Spirit Whisperer: Chronicles of a Medium

Bridging Two Realms

www.johnholland.com

Lysa Mateau

Psychic Diaries

www.channelingspirits.net

Kim Russo

The Happy Medium: Life Lessons from the Other Side

www.kimthehappymedium.com

Suzan Saxman

The Reluctant Psychic: A Memoir

www.suzanfionasaxman.com

James Van Praagh

Talking to Heaven

www.vanpraagh.com

Michelle Whitedove

> *She Talks with Angels*

> www.michellewhitedove.com

Lisa Williams

> *The Survival of the Soul*

> *Life Among the Dead*

> www.lisawilliams.com

Chakras

Tori Hartman

> *Chakra Wisdom Oracle Cards*

> *How to Read Cards for Yourself and Others*

> www.torihartman.com

Margaret Ann Lembo

> *Chakra Awakening*

> www.margaretannlembo.com

Crystals

Judy Hall

> *The Crystal Bible*

> *Encyclopedia of Crystals*

Crystal Prescriptions

Margaret Ann Lembo

The Essential Guide to Aromatherapy and Vibrational Healing

The Essential Guide to Crystals, Minerals and Stones

Color Your Life with Stones

www.margaretannlembo.com

Melody

Love is in the Earth

www.loveisintheearth.org

Bloom Post

Plant Spirit Totems: Connecting with the Wisdom of the Plant Kingdom

Shaman's Toolbox: Practical Tools for Powerful Transformation

www.bloompost.com

Robert Simmons/Naisha Ahsian

The Book of Stones: Who They Are and What They Teach

Earth Magic and Shamanism

Ted Andrews

> *Nature Speak*
>
> *Animal Speak*
>
> *Animal Wise*
>
> *Psychic Protection*

Scott Cunningham

> *Divination*
>
> *Earth Power*
>
> *The Complete Book of Incense, Oils, and Brews*
>
> *Encyclopedia of Magical Herbs*
>
> *Magical Herbalism*

Steven D. Farmer

> *Earth Magic*
>
> *Animal Spirit Guides*
>
> www.earthmagic.net

Paul Francis

> *The Shamanic Journey*

Michael Harner

> *The Way of the Shaman*

Sandra Ingerman

> *Shamanic Journeying*

> *Walking in the Light*

> *Soul Retrieval: Mending the Fragmented Self*

> www.sandraingerman.com

Mystery Schools and Education

Academy of Mystical Arts and Sciences with Kala Ambrose – www.exploreyourspirit.com/academy

Sandy Anastasi – www.sandyanastasi.com

Evolve with John Edward – www.johnedward.net/evolve

Tori Hartman--www.torihartman.com

Hans King – www.hansking.com/intuitive_development

Loner Wolf--www.lonerwolf.com

Omega Institute for Holistic Studies – www.eomega.org

Tarot Academy and Tarot Summer School - www.ethony.com

The Reader's Studio – www.tarotschool.com

Herman Siu – www.hermansiu.com
YouTube channel
https://www.youtube.com/channel/UCxsFOajYrC
Y6-1DWECBqJKQ

Spiritual Arts Institute – www.spiritualarts.org

Tarot Readers Academy – www.ethony.com

James Van Praagh School of Mystical Arts –
www.jvpschoolofmysticalarts.com

Lisa Williams--www.lisawilliams.com

Numerology

Michelle Buchman

> *The Numerology Guidebook*

> www.michellebuchanan.co.nz

Glynis McCants

> *Glynis Has Your Number*

> *Love in the Numbers*

> www.glynishasyournumber.com

Lloyd Strayhorn

> *Numbers and You: A Numerology Guide to
> Everyday Living*

> *Lloyd's Book of Numbers*

www.lloyd-strayhorn.com

Pendulum

Raymon Grace

> *The Future is Yours: Do Something About It*

> *Techniques That Work for Me*

> www.raymongrace.us

Erich Hunter

> *Pendulum Master (with Raymon Grace)*

> *Pendulum Healing*

> *Advanced Pendulum Healing*

> www.erichhunter.com

Dale W. Olson

> *The Pendulum Instruction Chart Book*

> www.getintuitive.com

Richard Webster

> *Dowsing for Beginners*

> *Pendulum Magic for Beginners*

> www.richardwebster.co.nz

Prayer

Anne Lamont

> *Help, Thanks, Wow*

John Edward

> *Practical Praying*

> www.johnedward.net

Psychic Development

Kala Ambrose

> *The Awakened Dreamer*

> *The Awakened Aura*

> *The Awakened Psychic*

> *9 Life Altering Lessons*

> www.exploreyourspirit.com

Sandy Anastasi

> *The Tarot Reader's Workbook*

> *Kabbala Pathworking*

> *The Anastasi System*

> *Astrology: Art and Science*

> www.sandyanastasi.com

Echo Bodine

A Still, Small Voice: A Psychic's Guide to Awakening Your Intuition

The Gift: Understand and Develop Your Psychic Abilities

Look for the Good ad You'll Find God: The Spiritual Journey of a Psychic and Healer

www.echobodine.com

Diane Brandon

Intuition for Beginners

Dream Interpretation for Beginners (a couple of my dreams were included in this one)

www.dianebrandon.com

Dr. Wayne W. Dyer

There's a Spiritual Solution to Every Problem

Change Your Thoughts, Change Your Life

I Can See Clearly Now

The Power of Intention

Wishes Fulfilled

John Edward

One Last Time

Infinite Quest

www.johnedward.net

Shakti Gawain

Creative Visualization

www.shaktigawain.com

Dr. Bruce Goldberg

New Age Hypnosis

Spirit Guide Contact Through Hypnosis

Soul Healing

www.drbrucegoldberg.com

Louise Hay

You Can Heal Your Life

Heal Your Body

Hans Christian King

Guided

www.hansking.com

Barbara Y. Martin

Aura Life

Change Your Aura, Change Your Life

Communing with the Divine, Karma and Reincarnation

The Healing Power of Your Aura

www.spiritarts.com

Lysa Mateau

Psychic Diaries

www.channelingspirits.com

Dr. Joseph Murphy

The Power of the Subconscious Mind

Carolyn Myss

Anatomy of the Spirit: The Seven Stages of Power and Healing

Sacred Contracts: Awakening Your Divine Potential

Invisible Acts of Power: Channeling Grace in Your Everyday Life

Entering the Castle: Finding the Inner Path to God and Your Soul's Purpose

Why People Don't Heal and How They Can

www.myss.com

Aphrodette North – Inner Mysteries Profiled

    On Blog Talk Radio

    www.aphrodette.com

Elizabeth Claire Prophet

    Violet Flame to Heal Body, Mind, and Soul

Gary E. Schwartz

    The Afterlife Experiments

    The God Experiments

    The Sacred Promise

    www.drgaryschwartz.com

Dr. Brian Weiss

    Many Lives, Many Masters

    Through Time into Healing

    Only Love is Real

    Messages from the Masters

    Same Soul, Many Bodies

    Miracles Happen

    Meditation

    www.brianweiss.com

Michelle Whitedove

Ask Whitedove

Angels are Talking

She Talks to Angels

Ghost Stalker

www.michellewhitedove.com

Stuart Wilde

Miracles

Infinite Self

The Force

Affirmations

The Quickening

Silent Power

Sixth Sense

www.stuartwilde.com

Anthony Williams

Medical Medium

Life Changing Foods

Thyroid Healing

Liver Rescue

www.medicalmedium.com

Lisa Williams

Was That A Sign from Heaven?

www.lisawilliams.com

John Zaffis

Shadows of the Dark

Demon Haunted

Haunted by the Things You Love

www.johnzaffis.com

Psychic Protection

Kala Ambrose

Awakened Aura

Ted Andrews

Psychic Protection

Draja Mickaharic

Spiritual Cleansings: A Handbook of Psychic Protection

Christopher Penczak

The Witches Shield

Sophie Reicher

>*Spiritual Protection*

Benebell Wen

>*Protection*

>www.benebellwen.com

Psychology

John Friedlander and Gloria Hemsher

>*Psychic Psychology*

>www.psychicpsychology.org

Dr. Bruce Lipton

>*The Biology of Belief: Unleashing the Power of Consciousness, Matter & Miracles*

>*The Honeymoon Effect: The Science of Creating Heaven on Earth*

>www.brucelipton.com

Dr. Joseph Murphy

>*The Power of the Subconscious Mind*

Reiki Healing

Penelope Quest

Reiki for Life

The Reiki Manual (with Kathy Roberts)

www.reiki-quest.co.uk

Diane Stein

Essential Reiki

www.dianestein.net

Dr. Mikao Usui

The Original Reiki Handbook

Tarot

Brigit Esselmont

Everyday Tarot

www.biddytarot.com

Ethony

www.ethony.com

Tarot Academy and Tarot Summer School

Marcus Katz and Tali Goodwin

Tarosophy: Tarot to Engage in Life, Not Escape It

Around the Tarot in 78 Days

      Tarot Face to Face

      Secrets of the Waite-Smith Tarot

      www.tarotprofessionals.com

Corrine Kenner

      Tarot Journaling

      Tarot for Writers

      Tarot and Astrology

      www.corrinekenner.com

Galaxy Tarot App on Google Play or

      www.galaxytone.com/galaxytarot/

Eden Gray

      The Complete Guide to the Tarot

      Mastering the Tarot

Mary K. Greer

      21 Ways to Read a Tarot Card

      Understanding the Tarot Court

      The Complete Book of Tarot Reversals

      Tarot for Your Self

      www.marykgreer.com

125

Tori Hartman

>   *How to Learn to Read Tarot in an Hour*
>
>   *12 Step Tarot*
>
>   www.torihartman.com

Anthony Louis

>   *Tarot Plain and Simple*
>
>   *Tarot Beyond the Basics*
>
>   *Llewellyn's Complete Book of Tarot*
>
>   www.tonylouis.wordpress.com

Barbara Moore

>   *Tarot for Beginners: A Practical Guide to Reading Cards*
>
>   *Your Tarot Your Way: Learn to Read with Any Deck*
>
>   *Tarot Made Easy: Your Tarot Your Way*
>
>   *Tarot Spread: Layouts & Techniques to Empower Your Readings*
>
>   www.tarotshaman.com

Rachel Pollack

>   *78 Degrees of Wisdom*

Tarot Wisdom: Spiritual Teachings and Deeper Meanings

The New Tarot Handbook

The Forest of Souls

Complete Illustrated Guide to the Tarot

www.rachelpollack.com

Theresa Reed

The Tarot Coloring Book

www.thetarotlady.com

Benebell Wen

Holistic Tarot

The Tao of Craft

www.benebellwen.com

Acknowledgments

I've lost count of the many teachers I've had in metaphysics. Many blessings to all who have paved the path to the mainstream. I have included many of their books and websites in the Suggested Reading and Resources.

But I've learned the most from the folks I've had the pleasure of reading with in the past twenty years. I hope you find that exchange of energy reflected here.

Special thanks to my editorial team, Rachel James and Debra Slack.

About the Author

Sheila Englehart is an author and practical tarot reader in North Carolina. She left the corporate sector to practice hypnotherapy, write two novels in the paranormal genre, and reads psychology-based tarot. She is a member of the American Tarot Association and Tarot Professionals, U.K.

If you would like to receive notifications of future releases, please email:

sheilaenglehart@gmail.com

Finally

If you've gained helpful knowledge from this book, I would greatly appreciate your leaving a review on the online outlet you purchased from.

Many blessings!

48938583R00076

Made in the USA
Columbia, SC
17 January 2019